INTERESTING QUOTES

PRANJAL BORKAR

Contents

1

MOTIVATIONAL QUOTES

1."If you want to achieve greatness stop asking for permission." --Anonymous

2. "Things work out best for those who make the best of how things work out." --John Wooden

3. "To live a creative life, we must lose our fear of being wrong." --Anonymous

4. "If you are not willing to risk the usual you will have to settle for the ordinary." --Jim Rohn

5. "Trust because you are willing to accept the risk, not because it's safe or certain." --

Anonymous

6. "Take up one idea. Make that one idea your life--think of it, dream of it, live on that idea. Let the brain, muscles, nerves, every part of your body, be full of that idea, and just leave every other idea alone. This is the way to success." --Swami Vivekananda

7. "All our dreams can come true if we have the courage to pursue them." --Walt Disney

8. "Good things come to people who wait, but better things come to those who go out and get them." --Anonymous

9. "If you do what you always did, you will get what you always got." --Anonymous

10. "Success is walking from failure to failure with no loss of enthusiasm." --Winston Churchill

11. "Just when the caterpillar thought the world was ending, he turned into a butterfly." --Proverb

12. "Successful entrepreneurs are givers and not takers of positive energy." --Anonymous

13. "Whenever you see a successful person you only see the public glories, never the private sacrifices to reach them." --Vaibhav Shah

14. "Opportunities don't happen, you create them." --Chris Grosser

15. "Try not to become a person of success, but rather try to become a person of value." --Albert Einstein

16. "Great minds discuss ideas; average minds discuss events; small minds discuss people." --Eleanor Roosevelt

17. "I have not failed. I've just found 10,000 ways that won't work." --Thomas A. Edison

18. "If you don't value your time, neither will others. Stop giving away your time and talents--start charging for it." --Kim Garst

19. "A successful man is one who can lay a firm foundation with the bricks others have thrown at him." --David Brinkley

20. "No one can make you feel inferior without your consent." --Eleanor Roosevelt

21. "The whole secret of a successful life is to find out what is one's destiny to do, and then do it." --Henry Ford

22. "If you're going through hell keep going." --Winston Churchill

23. "The ones who are crazy enough to think they can change the world, are the ones who do." --Anonymous

24. "Don't raise your voice, improve your argument." --Anonymous

25. "What seems to us as bitter trials are often blessings in disguise." --Oscar Wilde

26. "The meaning of life is to find your gift. The purpose of life is to give it away." --Anonymous

27. "The distance between insanity and genius is measured only by success." --Bruce Feirstein

28. "When you stop chasing the wrong things, you give the right things a chance to catch you." --Lolly Daskal

29. "I believe that the only courage anybody ever needs is the courage to follow your own dreams." --Oprah Winfrey

30. "No masterpiece was ever created by a lazy artist." --Anonymous

31. "Happiness is a butterfly, which when pursued, is always beyond your grasp, but which, if you will sit down quietly, may alight upon you." --Nathaniel Hawthorne

32. "If you can't explain it simply, you don't understand it well enough." --Albert Einstein

33. "Blessed are those who can give without remembering and take without forgetting." --Anonymous

34. "Do one thing every day that scares you." --Anonymous

35. "What's the point of being alive if you don't at least try to do something remarkable." --Anonymous

36. "Life is not about finding yourself. Life is about creating yourself." --Lolly Daskal

37. "Nothing in the world is more common than unsuccessful people with talent." --Anonymous

38. "Knowledge is being aware of what you can do. Wisdom is knowing when not to do it." --Anonymous

39. "Your problem isn't the problem. Your reaction is the problem." --Anonymous

40. "You can do anything, but not everything." --Anonymous

41. "Innovation distinguishes between a leader and a follower." --Steve Jobs

42. "There are two types of people who will tell you that you cannot make a difference in this world: those who are afraid to try and those who are afraid you will succeed." --Ray Goforth

43. "Thinking should become your capital asset, no matter whatever ups and downs you come across in your life." --A.P.J. Abdul Kalam

44. "I find that the harder I work, the more luck I seem to have." --Thomas Jefferson

45. "The starting point of all achievement is desire." --Napoleon Hill

46. "Success is the sum of small efforts, repeated day-in and day-out." --Robert Collier

47. "If you want to achieve excellence, you can get there today. As of this second, quit doing less-

than-excellent work." --Thomas J. Watson

48. "All progress takes place outside the comfort zone." --Michael John Bobak

49. "You may only succeed if you desire succeeding; you may only fail if you do not mind failing." --Philippos

50. "Courage is resistance to fear, mastery of fear--not absence of fear." --Mark Twain

51. "Only put off until tomorrow what you are willing to die having left undone." --Pablo Picasso

52. "People often say that motivation doesn't last. Well, neither does bathing--that's why we recommend it daily." --Zig Ziglar

53. "We become what we think about most of the time, and that's the strangest secret." --Earl Nightingale

54. "The only place where success comes before work is in the dictionary." --Vidal Sassoon

55. "Too many of us are not living our dreams because we are living our fears." --Les Brown

56. "I find that when you have a real interest in life and a curious life, that sleep is not the most important thing." --Martha Stewart

57. "It's not what you look at that matters, it's what you see." --Anonymous

58. "The road to success and the road to failure are almost exactly the same." --Colin R. Davis

59. "The function of leadership is to produce more leaders, not more followers." --Ralph Nader

60. "Success is liking yourself, liking what you do, and liking how you do it." --Maya Angelou

61. "As we look ahead into the next century, leaders will be those who empower others." --Bill Gates

62. "A real entrepreneur is somebody who has no safety net underneath them." --Henry Kravis

63. "The first step toward success is taken when you refuse to be a captive of the environment in which you first find yourself." --Mark Caine

64. "People who succeed have momentum. The more they succeed, the more they want to succeed, and the more they find a way to succeed. Similarly, when someone is failing, the tendency is to get on a downward spiral that can even become a self-fulfilling prophecy." --Tony Robbins

65. "When I dare to be powerful, to use my strength in the service of my vision, then it becomes less and less important whether I am afraid." --Audre Lorde

66. "Whenever you find yourself on the side of the majority, it is time to pause and reflect." --Mark Twain

67. "The successful warrior is the average man, with laser-like focus." --Bruce Lee

68. "There is no traffic jam along the extra mile." --Roger Staubach

69. "Develop success from failures. Discouragement and failure are two of the surest stepping stones to success." --Dale Carnegie

70. "If you don't design your own life plan, chances are you'll fall into someone else's plan. And guess what they have planned for you? Not much." --Jim Rohn

71. "If you genuinely want something, don't wait for it--teach yourself to be impatient." --Gurbaksh Chahal

72. "Don't let the fear of losing be greater than the excitement of winning." --Robert Kiyosaki

73. "If you want to make a permanent change, stop focusing on the size of your problems and start focusing on the size of you!" --T. Harv Eker

74. "You can't connect the dots looking forward; you can only connect them looking backwards. So you have to trust that the dots will somehow connect in your future. You have to trust in something--your gut, destiny, life, karma, whatever. This approach has never let me down, and it has made all the difference in my life." --Steve Jobs

75. "Two roads diverged in a wood and I took the one less traveled by, and that made all the difference." --Robert Frost

76. "The number one reason people fail in life is because they listen to their friends, family, and neighbors." --Napoleon Hill

77. "The reason most people never reach their goals is that they don't define them, or ever seriously consider them as believable or achievable. Winners can tell you where they are going, what they plan to do along the way, and who will be sharing the adventure with them." --Denis Waitley

78. "In my experience, there is only one motivation, and that is desire. No reasons or principle contain it or stand against it." --Jane Smiley

79. "Success does not consist in never making mistakes but in never making the same one a second time." --George Bernard Shaw

80. "I don't want to get to the end of my life and find that I lived just the length of it. I want to have lived the width of it as well." --Diane Ackerman

81. "You must expect great things of yourself before you can do them." --Michael Jordan

82. "Motivation is what gets you started. Habit is what keeps you going." --Jim Ryun

83. "People rarely succeed unless they have fun in what they are doing." --Dale Carnegie

84. "There is no chance, no destiny, no fate, that can hinder or control the firm resolve of a determined soul." --Ella Wheeler Wilcox

85. "Our greatest fear should not be of failure but of succeeding at things in life that don't really matter." --Francis Chan

86. "You've got to get up every morning with determination if you're going to go to bed with satisfaction." --George Lorimer

87. "A goal is not always meant to be reached; it often serves simply as something to aim at." --Bruce Lee

88. "Success is ... knowing your purpose in life, growing to reach your maximum potential, and sowing seeds that benefit others." --John C. Maxwell

89. "Be miserable. Or motivate yourself. Whatever has to be done, it's always your choice." --Wayne Dyer

90. "To accomplish great things, we must not only act, but also dream, not only plan, but also

believe." --Anatole France

91. "Most of the important things in the world have been accomplished by people who have kept on trying when there seemed to be no help at all." --Dale Carnegie

92. "You measure the size of the accomplishment by the obstacles you had to overcome to reach your goals." --Booker T. Washington

93. "Real difficulties can be overcome; it is only the imaginary ones that are unconquerable." --Theodore N. Vail

94. "It is better to fail in originality than to succeed in imitation." --Herman Melville

95. "What would you do if you weren't afraid." --Spencer Johnson

96. "Little minds are tamed and subdued by misfortune; but great minds rise above it." --Washington Irving

97. "Failure is the condiment that gives success its flavor." --Truman Capote

98. "Don't let what you cannot do interfere with what you can do." --John R. Wooden

99. "You may have to fight a battle more than once to win it." --Margaret Thatcher

100. "A man can be as great as he wants to be. If you believe in yourself and have the courage, the determination, the dedication, the competitive drive and if you are willing to sacrifice the little things in life and pay the price for the things that are worthwhile, it can be done." --Vince Lombardi

2

HAPPINESS QUOTES

1. "Happiness depends upon ourselves." —Aristotle

2. "To be kind to all, to like many and love a few, to be needed and wanted by those we love, is certainly the nearest we can come to happiness." —Mary Stuart

3. "Happiness is not something ready-made. It comes from your own actions." —Dalai Lama

4. "If you want happiness for an hour—take a nap. If you want happiness for a day—go fishing. If you want happiness for a year—inherit a fortune. If you want happiness for a

lifetime—help someone else." —Chinese Proverb

5. "It's a helluva start, being able to recognize what makes you happy." —Lucille Ball

6. "Don't underestimate the value of Doing Nothing, of just going along, listening to all the things you can't hear, and not bothering." —Winnie the Pooh

7. "Some cause happiness wherever they go; others whenever they go." —Oscar Wilde

8. "Happiness is not in the mere possession of money; it lies in the joy of achievement, in the thrill of creative effort." —Franklin D. Roosevelt

9. "It's been my experience that you can nearly always enjoy things if you make up your mind firmly that you will." —L.M. Montgomery

10. "Since you get more joy out of giving joy to others, you should put a good deal of thought into the happiness that you are able to give." —Eleanor Roosevelt

11. "Very little is needed to make a happy life; it is all within yourself, in your way of thinking." —Marcus Aurelius Antoninus

12. "I'd far rather be happy than right any day." —Douglas Adams

13. "The foolish man seeks happiness in the distance, the wise grows it under his feet." —James Oppenheim

14. "Happiness is nothing more than good health and a bad memory." —Albert Schweitzer

15. "I, not events, have the power to make me happy or unhappy today. I can choose which it shall be. Yesterday is dead, tomorrow hasn't arrived yet. I have just one day, today, and I'm going to be happy in it." —Groucho Marx

16. "If someone bases his/her happiness on major events like a great job, huge amounts of money, a flawlessly happy marriage or a trip to Paris, that person isn't going to be happy much of the time. If, on the other hand, happiness depends on a good breakfast, flowers in the yard, a drink or a nap, then we are more likely to live

with quite a bit of happiness." —Andy Rooney

17. "The first recipe for happiness is: avoid too lengthy meditation on the past." —Andre Maurois

18. "Let us be grateful to the people who make us happy; they are the charming gardeners who make our souls blossom." —Marcel Proust

19. "Most people are about as happy as they make up their minds to be." —Abraham Lincoln

20. "If you look to others for fulfillment, you will never be fulfilled. If your happiness depends on money, you will never be happy with yourself. Be content with what you have; rejoice in the way things are. When you realize there is nothing lacking, the world belongs to you." —Lao Tzu

21. "If you want to be happy, set a goal that commands your thoughts, liberates your energy, and inspires your hopes." —Andrew Carnegie

22. "Tension is who you think you should be, relaxation is who you are." —Chinese Proverb

23. "Happiness is not a station you arrive at, but a manner of traveling." —Margaret Lee Runbeck

24. "Thousands of candles can be lit from a single candle, and the life of the candle will not be shortened. Happiness never decreases by being shared." —Buddha (101 Buddha Quotes)

25. "True happiness is not attained through self-gratification, but through fidelity to a worthy purpose." —Helen Keller

26. "Blessed are those who can give without remembering and take without forgetting." —Bernard Meltzer

27. "Even a happy life cannot be without a measure of darkness, and the word happy would lose its meaning if it were not balanced by sadness. It is far better to take things as they come along with patience and equanimity." —Carl Jung

28. "When one door of happiness closes, another opens, but often we look so long at the closed door that we do not see the one that has been opened for us." —Helen Keller

29. "Success is getting what you want. Happiness is wanting what you get." —Dale Carnegie

30. "We all get report cards in many different ways, but the real excitement of what you're doing is in the doing of it. It's not what you're gonna get in the end—it's not the final curtain—it's really in the doing it, and loving what you're doing." —Ralph Lauren

31. "The happiness of life is made up of the little charities of a kiss or smile, a kind look, a heartfelt compliment." —Samuel Taylor Coleridge

32. "Far better is it to dare mighty things, to win glorious triumphs–even though checkered by failure–than to rank with those poor spirits who neither enjoy much nor suffer much, because they live in a gray twilight that knows not victory nor defeat." —Theodore Roosevelt

33. "Happiness is when what you think, what you say, and what you do are in harmony." —Mahatma Gandhi

34. "There's nothing like deep breaths after laughing that hard. Nothing in the world like a sore stomach for the right reasons." —Stephen Chbosky

35. "Count your age by friends, not years. Count your life by smiles, not tears." —John Lennon

36. "If more of us valued food and cheer and song above hoarded gold, it would be a merrier world." —J.R.R. Tolkien

37. "The most important thing is to enjoy your life—to be happy—it's all that matters." —Audrey Hepburn

38. "Happiness is a warm puppy." —Charles M. Schulz

39. "Happiness is holding someone in your arms and knowing you hold the whole world." —Orhan Pamuk

40. "All happiness depends on courage and work." —Honoré de Balzac

41. "Let no one ever come to you without leaving better and happier." —Mother Teresa

42. "So we shall let the reader answer this question for himself: who is the happier man, he who has braved the storm of life and lived or he who has stayed securely on shore and merely existed?" —Hunter S. Thompson

43. "Now and then it's good to pause in our pursuit of happiness and just be happy." —Guillaume Apollinaire

44. "The happiness of your life depends upon the quality of your thoughts." —Marcus Aurelius

45. "Happiness is not the absence of problems, it's the ability to deal with them." —Steve Maraboli

46. "Those who are not looking for happiness are the most likely to find it, because those who are searching forget that the surest way to be happy

is to seek happiness for others." —Martin Luther King Jr.

47. "I'm choosing happiness over suffering, I know I am. I'm making space for the unknown future to fill up my life with yet-to-come surprises." —Elizabeth Gilbert

48. "True happiness is to enjoy the present, without anxious dependence upon the future, not to amuse ourselves with either hopes or fears but to rest satisfied with what we have, which is sufficient, for he that is so wants nothing. The greatest blessings of mankind are within us and within our reach. A wise man is content with his lot, whatever it may be, without wishing for what he has not." —Seneca

49. "Whoever is happy will make others happy." —Anne Frank

50. "The greater part of our happiness or misery depends upon our dispositions, and not upon our circumstances." —Martha Washington

51. "Happiness is not a possession to be prized, it is a quality of thought, a state of mind." —Daphne du Maurier

52. "Letting go gives us freedom, and freedom is the only condition for happiness. If, in our heart, we still cling to anything – anger, anxiety, or possessions – we cannot be free." —Thich Nhat Hanh

53. "The power of finding beauty in the humblest things makes home happy and life lovely." —Louisa May Alcott

54. "Action may not always bring happiness, but there is no happiness without action. " —William James

55. "If only we'd stop trying to be happy, we could have a pretty good time." —Edith Wharton

56. "Happiness is a risk. If you're not a little scared, then you're not doing it right." —Sarah Addison Allen

57. "The more you praise and celebrate your life, the more there is in life to celebrate." —Oprah

Winfrey

58. "All I ask is one thing, and I'm asking this particularly of young people: please don't be cynical. I hate cynicism, for the record, it's my least favorite quality and it doesn't lead anywhere. Nobody in life gets exactly what they thought they were going to get. But if you work really hard and you're kind, amazing things will happen." —Conan O'Brien

59. "There is no happiness like that of being loved by your fellow creatures, and feeling that your presence is an addition to their comfort." —Charlotte Brontë

60. "There is only one way to happiness and that is to cease worrying about things which are beyond the power or our will. " —Epictetus

61. "Happiness is a perfume you cannot pour on others without getting some on yourself." —Ralph Waldo Emerson

62. "Everyone wants to live on top of the mountain, but all the happiness and growth occurs while you're climbing it." —Andy Rooney

63. "Just because you are happy it does not mean that the day is perfect but that you have looked beyond its imperfections" —Bob Marley

64. "One must believe in the possibility of happiness in order to be happy." —Leo Tolstoy

65. "The secret of happiness is not in doing what one likes, but in liking what one does." —J.M. Barrie

66. "[F]or just one second, look at your life and see how perfect it is. Stop looking for the next secret door that is going to lead you to your real life. Stop waiting. This is it: there's nothing else. It's here, and you'd better decide to enjoy it or you're going to be miserable wherever you go, for the rest of your life, forever." —Lev Grossman

67. "Happiness only real when shared." —Christopher McCandless

68. "You must be the best judge of your own happiness." —Jane Austen

69. "One is happy as a result of one's own efforts once one knows the necessary ingredients of happiness: simple tastes, a certain degree of courage, self-denial to a point, love of work, and above all, a clear conscience." —George Sand

70. "There is a kind of happiness and wonder that makes you serious. It is too good to waste on jokes." —C.S. Lewis

71. "The reason people find it so hard to be happy is that they always see the past better than it was, the present worse than it is, and the future less resolved than it will be." —Marcel Pagnol

72. "I shall take the heart. For brains do not make one happy, and happiness is the best thing in the world." —L. Frank Baum

73. "My happiness grows in direct proportion to my acceptance, and in inverse proportion to my expectations." —Michael J. Fox

74. "You can't buy happiness" —Kurt Cobain

75. "Most people would rather be certain they're miserable, than risk being happy." —Robert

Anthony

76. "Happiness is a choice that requires effort at times." —Aeschylus

77. "I do not think we have a 'right' to happiness. If happiness happens, say thanks." —Marlene Dietrich

78. "Of all the means to insure happiness throughout the whole life, by far the most important is the acquisition of friends." —Epicurus

79. "Got no checkbooks, got no banks. Still I'd like to express my thanks—I've got the sun in the mornin' and the moon at night." —Irving Berlin

80. "Do not look for happiness outside yourself. The awakened seek happiness inside." —Peter Deunov

81. "Why should we build our happiness on the opinons of others, when we can find it in our own hearts?" —Jean-Jacques Rousseau

82. "A flower blossoms for its own joy." —Oscar Wilde

83. "Happiness is like those palaces in fairytales whose gates are guarded by dragons: We must fight in order to conquer it." —Alexandre Dumas

84. "Some day you will find out that there is far more happiness in another's happiness than in your own." —Honoré de Balzac

85. "Happiness and confidence are the prettiest things you can wear" —Taylor Swift

86. "Laughter is a sunbeam of the soul." —Thomas Mann

87. "The thing everyone should realize is that the key to happiness is being happy for yourself and yourself." —Ellen DeGeneres

88. "The supreme happiness of life is the conviction that we are loved." —Victor Hugo

89. "Why not seize the pleasure at once? — How often is happiness destroyed by preparation, foolish preparation!" —Jane Austen

90. "I needed to stop being what everyone thought I was." —Sarah Addison Allen

91. "It is necessary to the happiness of man that he be mentally faithful to himself. Infidelity does not consist in believing, or in disbelieving, it consists in professing to believe what he does not believe." —Thomas Paine

92. "Happiness is a gift and the trick is not to expect it, but to delight in it when it comes." —Charles Dickens

93. "Happiness doesn't come from achievements, or money, or any sort of treasure. Happiness is a frame of mind, not a destination. It's appreciating what you've got and building relationships with those around you." —Janette Rallison

94. "If you want to find happiness, find gratitude." —Steve Maraboli

95. "The secret of a happy life is respect. Respect for yourself and respect for others." —Ayad Akhtar

96. "Happiness comes from living as you need to, as you want to. As your inner voice tells you to. Happiness comes from being who you actually are instead of who you think you are supposed to be." —Shonda Rhimes

97. "We are all happy if we but knew it." —Fyodor Dostoyevsky

98. "It is essential to happiness that our way of living should spring from our own deep impulses and not from the accidental tastes and desires of those who happen to be our neighbors, or even our relations." —Bertrand Russell

99. "I've learned ....That when you harbor bitterness, happiness will dock elsewhere." —Andy Rooney

100. "You have to be willing to get happy about nothing." —Andy Warhol

3 PEACE QUOTES

1. "Peace begins with a smile." — Mother Teresa

2. "Nothing can bring you peace but yourself. Nothing can bring you peace but the triumph of principles." — Ralph Waldo Emerson

3. "Do not let the behavior of others destroy your inner peace." — Dalai Lama

4. "An eye for an eye will only make the whole world blind." — Mahatma Gandhi

5. "You may say I'm a dreamer, but I'm not the only one. I hope someday you'll join us. And the world will live as one." — John Lennon, Imagine

6. "You cannot find peace by avoiding life." — Michael Cunningham, The Hours

7. "Peace cannot be kept by force; it can only be achieved by understanding." — Albert Einstein

8. "When you do the right thing, you get the feeling of peace and serenity associated with it. Do it again and again." — Roy T. Bennett

9. "Peace comes from within. Do not seek it without." — Siddhārtha Gautama

10. "You have peace when you make it with yourself." — Mitch Albom, The Five People You Meet in Heaven

11. "If you are depressed, you are living in the past. If you are anxious, you are living in the future. If you are at peace, you are living in the present." — Lao Tzu

12. "Peace is a daily, a weekly, a monthly process, gradually changing opinions, slowly eroding old barriers, quietly building new structures." —

President John F. Kennedy

13. "Peace is always beautiful." — Walt Whitman, Leaves of Grass

14. "It is not enough to win a war; it is more important to organize the peace." — Aristotle

15. "When you make peace with yourself, you make peace with the world."— Maha Ghosananda

16. "The practice of forgiveness is our most important contribution to the healing of the world." — Marianne Williamson

17. "There are two ways of spreading light: to be the candle or the mirror that reflects it." — Edith Wharton

18. "Learning to distance yourself from all the negativity is one of the greatest lessons to achieve inner peace." — Roy T. Bennett, The Light in the Heart

19. "Love is the purest form of a soul at peace." — Matthew Donnelly

20. "The day I understood everything, was the day I stopped trying to figure everything out. The day I knew peace was the day I let everything go." — C. JoyBell C.

21. "You should feel beautiful and you should feel safe. What you surround yourself with should bring you peace of mind and peace of spirit." — Stacy London

22. "If you cannot find peace within yourself, you will never find it anywhere else." — Marvin Gaye

23. "Peace is not something you wish for. It is something you make, something you are, something you do, and something you give away." — Robert Fulghum

24. "Until he extends the circle of his compassion to all living things, man will not himself find peace." — Albert Schweitzer

25. "Let go of the thoughts that don't make you strong." — Karen Salmansohn

26. "If you want to make peace with your enemy, you have to work with your enemy. Then he becomes your partner." — Nelson Mandela

27. "Many people think excitement is happiness... But when you are excited, you are not peaceful. True happiness is based on peace." — Thich Nhat Hanh, The Art of Power

28. "You cannot shake hands with a clenched fist."— Indira Gandhi

29. "Peace is the only battle worth waging." — Albert Camus

30. "Peace is a journey of a thousand miles, and it must be taken one step at a time." — President Lyndon B. Johnson

31. "Darkness cannot drive out darkness; only light can do that. Hate cannot drive out hate; only love can do that." — Rev. Dr. Martin Luther King, Jr.

32. "If you don't know the guy on the other side of the world, love him anyway because he's just like you. He has the same dreams, the same hopes and fears. It's one world, pal. We're all neighbors." — Frank Sinatra

33. "Courage is the price that life exacts for granting peace." — Amelia Earhart

34. "Why can't people just sit and read books and be nice to each other?" — David Baldacci, The Camel Club

35. "Peace is liberty in tranquility." — Marcus Tullius Cicero

36. "To forgive is the highest, most beautiful form of love. In return, you will receive untold peace and happiness" — Robert Muller

37. "It isn't enough to talk about peace. One must believe in it. And it isn't enough to believe in it. One must work at it." — Eleanor Roosevelt

38. "Peace is a day-to-day problem, the product of a multitude of events and judgments. Peace is

not an 'is,' it is a 'becoming.'" — Haile Selassie

39. "You will find peace not by trying to escape your problems, but by confronting them courageously. You will find peace not in denial, but in victory." — J. Donald Walters

40. "Peace is not absence of conflict; it is the ability to handle conflict by peaceful means." — President Ronald Reagan

41. "Do your little bit of good where you are; it's those little bits of good put together that overwhelm the world." — Desmond Tutu

42. "I do not want the peace which passeth understanding, I want the understanding which bringeth peace." — Helen Keller

43. "Do not be afraid to take a chance on peace, to teach peace, to live peace... Peace will be the last word of history." — Pope John Paul II

44. "Peace is such hard work. Harder than war. It takes way more effort to forgive than to kill." — Rae Carson, The Bitter Kingdom

45. “In the midst of movement and chaos, keep stillness inside of you.” — Deepak Chopra

46. “Be selective in your battles. Sometimes peace is better than being right.” — Unknown

47, “Of all our dreams today, there is none more important—or so hard to realize—than that of peace in the world.” — Lester B. Pearson

48. “Worrying does not take away tomorrow’s troubles. It takes away today’s peace.” — Randy Armstrong

49. “Peace is not the highest goal in life. It is the most fundamental requirement.” — Sadhguru

50. “World peace can be achieved when, in each person, the power of love replaces the love of power.” — Sri Chinmoy

51. “You can’t separate peace from freedom because no one can be at peace unless he has his freedom.” — Malcolm X

52. "There is no way to peace, peace is the way." — J. Muste

53. "Peace is not only better than war but infinitely more arduous." — George Bernard Shaw

54. "Never be in a hurry; do everything quietly and in a calm spirit. Do not lose your inner peace for anything whatsoever, even if your whole world seems upset." — Saint Francis de Sales

55. "Those who are free of resentful thoughts surely find peace." — Buddha

56. "Gratitude makes sense of our past, brings peace for today, and creates a vision for tomorrow." — Melody Beattie

57. "If there's no inner peace, people can't give it to you. The husband can't give it to you. Your children can't give it to you. You have to give it to you." — Linda Evans

58. "Promise yourself to be so strong that nothing can disturb your peace of mind." — Christian D. Larson

59. "Choose. The single clenched fist lifted and ready, or the open hand, held out and waiting. Choose: For we meet by one or the other." — Carl Sandburg

60. "There never was a good war or a bad peace." — Benjamin Franklin

61. "You find peace not by rearranging the circumstances of your life, but by realizing who you are at the deepest level." — Eckhart Tolle

62. "Peace is something we must all work for, every day, in every country." — Ban Ki-moon

63. "Everyone thinks of changing the world, but no one thinks of changing himself." — Leo Tolstoy

64. "Success is peace of mind which is a direct result of self-satisfaction in knowing you did your best to become the best you are capable of becoming." — John Wooden

65, "If you have a common purpose and an environment in which people want to help others succeed, the problems will be fixed quickly." — Alan Mulally

66. "If the human race wishes to have a prolonged and indefinite period of material prosperity, they have only got to behave in a peaceful and helpful way toward one another." — Winston Churchill

67. "Run to the rescue with love, and peace will follow." — River Phoenix

68. "If you want to end the war, then instead of sending guns, send books. Instead of sending tanks, send pens. Instead of sending soldiers, send teachers."— Malala Yousafzai

69. "When you find peace within yourself, you become the kind of person who can live at peace with others." — Peace Pilgrim

70. "I think it's naive to pray for world peace if we're not going to change the form in which we live." — Godfrey Reggio

71. "The only alternative to war is peace and the only road to peace is negotiations."— Golda Meir

72. "Peace by persuasion has a pleasant sound, but I think we should not be able to work it. We should have to tame the human race first, and history seems to show that that cannot be done." — Mark Twain, The Complete Letters of Mark Twain

73. "Peace only comes from accepting the inevitable and taming our desires." — The Ancient Sage

74. "Peace is the result of retraining your mind to process life as it is, rather than as you think it should be." — Wayne W. Dyer, There's a Spiritual Solution to Every Problem

75. "Peace, which costs nothing, is attended with infinitely more advantage than any victory with all its expense." — Thomas Paine, The Rights of

Man

76. "We don't realize that, somewhere within us all, there does exist a supreme self who is eternally at peace." — Elizabeth Gilbert, Eat, Pray, Love

77. "Not one of us can rest, be happy, be at home, be at peace with ourselves, until we end hatred and division." — Congressman John Lewis

78. "You'll never find peace of mind until you listen to your heart." — George Michael

79. "We will know peace the day we truly know ourselves." — Maxime Lagacé

80. "First keep the peace within yourself, then you can also bring peace to others." — Thomas á Kempis

81. "There is always a certain peace in being what one is, in being that completely." — Ugo Betti

82. "Make peace with your broken pieces." — Unknown

83. "Peace is costly, but it is worth the expense." — African proverb

84. "Only art and music have the power to bring peace." — Yoko Ono

85. "Peace is our gift to each other." — Elie Wiesel

86. "The best fighter is never angry." — Lao Tzu

87. "I am content; that is a blessing greater than riches; and he to whom that is given need ask no more." — Henry Fielding

88. "Inner peace can be reached only when we practice forgiveness. Forgiveness is letting go of the past and is therefore the means for correcting our misperceptions." — Gerald G. Jampolsky, Love is Letting Go of Fear

89. "Do not look for happiness outside yourself. The awakened seek happiness inside." — Peter

Deunov

90. "We are not at peace with others because we are not at peace with ourselves, and we are not at peace with ourselves because we are not at peace with God." — Thomas Merton

91. "Peace brings with it so many positive emotions that it is worth aiming for in all circumstances." — Estella Eliot

92. "Peace is the first thing the angels sang." — John Keble

93. "How far that little candle throws his beams! So shines a good deed in a weary world." — William Shakespeare, The Merchant of Venice

94. "For though my faith is not yours and your faith is not mine, if we are each free to light our own flame, together we can banish some of the darkness of the world." — Rabbi Lord Jonathan Sacks

95. "Peace comes from being able to contribute the best that we have, and all that we are, toward creating a world that supports everyone. But it is

also securing the space for others to contribute the best that they have and all that they are." — Hafsat Abiola

96. "Peace is more important than all justice; and peace was not made for the sake of justice, but justice for the sake of peace." — Ezra Taft Benson

97. "We will not have peace by afterthought." — Norman Cousins

98. "Good wishes alone will not ensure peace." — Alfred Nobel

99. "Peace is the umpire for doing the will of God." — Edwin Louis Cole

100. "You can find peace amidst the storms that threaten you." — Joseph B. Wirthlin

4

kindness quotes

“Kindness is your soul’s basic nature, acknowledge it and be kind.” ~ Invajy

“The smallest act of kindness is worth more than the greatest intention.” ~Kahlil Gibran

“When words are both true and kind, they can change the world.” ~ Buddha

“Be kind whenever possible. It is always possible.” ~ Dalai Lama

“Three things in human life are important. The first is to be kind. The second is to be kind. And the third is to be kind.” ~ Henry James

"Gratitude, compassion and kindness are pillars to make you a better person." ~ Invajy

"Kind words can be short and easy to speak but their echoes are truly endless." ~ Mother Teresa

"Beginning today, treat everyone you meet as if they were going to be dead by midnight. Extend to them all the care, kindness and understanding you can muster, and do it with no thought of any reward. Your life will never be the same again." ~ Og Mandino

"No one is born hating another person...People must learn to hate, and if they can learn to hate, they can be taught to love, for love comes more naturally to the human heart than its opposite." ~ Nelson Mandela

"Simple kindness may be the most vital key to the riddle of how human beings can live with each other in peace, and care properly for this planet we all share." ~ Bo Lozoff

"No kind action ever stops with itself. One kind action leads to another. Good example is followed. A single act of kindness throws out

roots in all directions, and the roots spring up and make new trees. The greatest work that kindness does to others is that it makes them kind themselves." ~ Amelia Earhart

"To practice five things under all circumstances constitutes perfect virtue; these five are gravity, generosity of soul, sincerity, earnestness, and kindness." ~ Confucius

"Carry out a random act of kindness, with no expectation of reward, safe in the knowledge that one day someone might do the same for you." ~ Princess Diana

"A smile remains the most inexpensive gift I can bestow on anyone and yet its powers can vanquish kingdoms." ~ Og Mandino

"Too often we underestimate the power of a touch, a smile, a kind word, a listening ear, an honest compliment, or the smallest act of caring, all of which have the potential to turn a life around." ~ Leo Buscaglia

"Never look down on anybody unless you're helping them up." ~ Jesse Jackson

"You can accomplish by kindness what you cannot by force." ~ Publilius Syrus

"No one has ever become poor by giving." ~ Anne Frank

"The beauty of a woman is not in a facial mole, but true beauty in a Woman is reflected in her soul. It is the caring that she lovingly gives, the passion that she knows." ~ Audrey Hepburn

"If you want to lift yourself up, lift someone else up." ~ Booker T. Washington

"Responsibility does not only lie with the leaders of our countries or with those who have been appointed or elected to do a particular job. It lies with each of us individually. Peace, for example, starts within each one of us. When we have inner peace, we can be at peace with those around us." ~ Dalai Lama

"A great man shows his greatness by the way he treats little men." ~ Thomas Carlyle

"Do your little bit of good where you are; it's those little bits of good put together that overwhelm the world." ~ Desmond Tutu

"Don't judge each day by the harvest you reap but by the seeds that you plant." ~ Robert Louis Stevenson

"How do we change the world? One random act of kindness at a time" ~ Morgan Freeman

"I've learned that people will forget what you said, people will forget what you did, but people will never forget how you made them feel." ~ Maya Angelou

"Courage. Kindness. Friendship. Character. These are the qualities that define us as human beings, and propel us, on occasion, to greatness." ~ J. Palacio

"One who knows how to show and to accept kindness will be a friend better than any possession." ~ Sophocles

"How would your life be different if... You stopped making negative judgmental

assumptions about people you encounter? Let today be the day...You look for the good in everyone you meet and respect their journey." ~ Steve Maraboli

"Be kind, for everyone you meet is fighting a battle you know nothing about." ~ Wendy Mass

"Kindness in words creates confidence. Kindness in thinking creates profoundness. And, kindness in giving creates love." ~ Lao Tzu

"Never be so busy as not to think of others." ~ Mother Teresa

"Gentleness and kindness will make our homes a paradise upon earth." ~ A. Bartol

"Kindness is the language which the deaf can hear and the blind can see." ~ Mark Twain

"We can't help everyone, but everyone can help someone." ~ Ronald Reagan

"Unexpected kindness is the most powerful, least costly, and most underrated agent of

human change." ~ Bob Kerrey

"I feel the capacity to care is the thing which gives life its deepest significance."- Pablo Casals

"Love and kindness are never wasted. They always make a difference. They bless the one who receives them, and they bless you, the giver." ~ Barbara De Angelis

"When you are kind to others, it not only changes you, it changes the world." ~ Harold Kushner

"Extend yourself in kindness to other human beings wherever you can." ~ Oprah Winfrey

"Human kindness has never weakened the stamina or softened the fiber of a free people. A nation does not have to be cruel to be tough." ~ Franklin Roosevelt

"Kindness and faithfulness keep a king safe, through kindness his throne is made secure." ~ King Solomon

"Because that's what kindness is. It's not doing something for someone else because they can't, but because you can." ~ Andrew Iskander

"Kindness begins with the understanding that we all struggle." ~ Charles Glassman

"Love and compassion are necessities, not luxuries. Without them, humanity cannot survive." ~ Dalai Lama

"Kindness and politeness are not overrated at all. They're underused." ~ Tommy Lee Jones

"My religion is very simple. My religion is kindness." ~Dalai Lama

"Wherever there is a human being, there is an opportunity for kindness." ~ Lucius Annaeus Seneca

"When we give cheerfully and accept gratefully, everyone is blessed." ~ Maya Angelou

"Genuine kindness is no ordinary act, but a gift of rare beauty." ~ Sylvia Rossetti

Kindness Quotes

"Kindness can become its own motive. We are made kind by being kind." ~ Eric Hoffer

"Practice random kindness and senseless acts of beauty." ~ Anne Herbert

"A kind gesture can reach a wound that only compassion can heal." ~ Steve Maraboli

"Compassion and daily acts of kindness make life far meaningful and fulfilling" Ĩnvajy

"What wisdom can you find that is greater than kindness?" ~ Jean-Jacques Rousseau

"Always be a little kinder than necessary." ~ James M. Barrie

"A kind word is like a Spring day." ~ Russian Proverb

"Kindness is the golden chain by which society is bound together." ~ Johann Wolfgang von Goethe

"Kindness is the only service that will stand the storm of life and not wash out. It will wear well and will be remembered long after the prism of politeness or the complexion of courtesy has faded away." ~ Abraham Lincoln

"When we feel love and kindness toward others, it not only makes others feel loved and cared for, but it helps us also to develop inner happiness and peace." ~ Dalai Lama

"Kindness is always fashionable, and always welcome." ~ Amelia Barr

"Tenderness and kindness are not signs of weakness and despair, but manifestations of strength and resolutions." ~ Kahlil Gibran

"What we all have in common is an appreciation of kindness and compassion; all the religions

have this. Love. We all lean towards love." ~ Richard Gere

"One thing I do know for a fact is that the nicer we are to our fellow human beings, the nicer the universe is to us." ~Joe Rogan

"To err on the side of kindness is seldom an error." ~ Liz Armbruster

A little thought and a little kindness are often worth more than a great deal of money." ~ John Ruskin

"Kindness is the sunshine in which virtue grows." ~ Robert Green Ingersoll

"Sometimes it takes only one act of kindness and caring to change a person's life." ~ Jackie Chan

"Gratitude is the inward feeling of kindness received. Thankfulness is the natural impulse to express that feeling. Thanksgiving is the following of that impulse." ~ Henry Van Dyke

"Kindness is a passport that opens doors and fashions friends. It softens hearts and molds relationships that can last lifetimes." ~ Joseph B. Wirthlin

"The words of kindness are more healing to a drooping heart than balm or honey." ~ Sarah Fielding

"Kindness is more important than wisdom, and the recognition of this is the beginning of wisdom." ~ Theodore Isaac Rubin

"Kindness makes you the most beautiful person in the world, no matter what you look like." ~ Anonymous

"Unless someone like you cares a whole awful lot, nothing is going to get better. It's not." ~ Dr. Seuss

"Constant kindness can accomplish much. As the sun makes ice melt, kindness causes misunderstanding, mistrust, and hostility to evaporate." ~ Albert Schweitzer

"No act of kindness, no matter how small, is ever wasted." ~ Aesop

"Kindness is the light that dissolves all walls between souls, families, and nations." ~ Paramahansa Yogananda

"Remember there's no such thing as a small act of kindness. Every act creates a ripple with no logical end." ~ Scott Adams

"Do things for people not because of who they are or what they do in return, but because of who you are." ~ Harold S. Kushner

"Forget injuries, never forget kindnesses." ~ Confucius

"The wonderful thing is that it's so incredibly easy to be kind." ~ Ingrid Newkirk

"An eye for an eye, and the whole world would be blind." ~ Kahlil Gibran

"I'm a big believer in acts of kindness, no matter how small." ~ Liam Neeson

"Deliberately seek opportunities for kindness, sympathy, and patience." ~ Evelyn Underhill

"You cannot do a kindness too soon, for you never know how soon it will be too late." ~ Ralph Waldo Emerson

"I've been searching for ways to heal myself, and I've found that kindness is the best way." ~ Lady Gaga

"Kindness is ever the begetter of kindness." ~ Sophocles

"If you have an impulse to kindness, act on it." ~ Douglas Coupland

"The everyday kindness of the back roads more than makes up for the acts of greed in the headlines." ~ Charles Kuralt

"A kindness received should be returned with a freer hand." ~ Saint Ambrose

"Kindness makes a fellow feel good whether it's being done to him or by him." ~ Frank A. Clark

"For attractive lips, speak words of kindness." ~ Audrey Hepburn

"Never lose a chance of saying a kind word." ~ William Makepeace Thackeray

"We make a living by what we get. We make a life by what we give." ~ Winston Churchill

5

Success quotes

1. “If you want to achieve greatness stop asking for permission.” —Anonymous

2. “Things work out best for those who make the best of how things work out.” —John Wooden

3. “To live a creative life, we must lose our fear of being wrong.” —Anonymous

4. “If you are not willing to risk the usual you will have to settle for the ordinary.” —Jim Rohn

5. “Trust because you are willing to accept the risk, not because it’s safe or certain.” —Anonymous

6. "Take up one idea. Make that one idea your life–think of it, dream of it, live on that idea. Let the brain, muscles, nerves, every part of your body, be full of that idea, and just leave every other idea alone. This is the way to success." —Swami Vivekananda

7. "All our dreams can come true if we have the courage to pursue them." —Walt Disney

8. "Good things come to people who wait, but better things come to those who go out and get them." —Anonymous

9. "If you do what you always did, you will get what you always got." —Anonymous

10. "Success is walking from failure to failure with no loss of enthusiasm." —Winston Churchill

11. "Just when the caterpillar thought the world was ending, he turned into a butterfly." —Proverb

12. "Successful entrepreneurs are givers and not takers of positive energy." —Anonymous

13. "Whenever you see a successful person you only see the public glories, never the private sacrifices to reach them." —Vaibhav Shah

14. "Opportunities don't happen, you create them." —Chris Grosser

15. "Try not to become a person of success, but rather try to become a person of value." —Albert Einstein

16. "Great minds discuss ideas; average minds discuss events; small minds discuss people." —Eleanor Roosevelt

17. "I have not failed. I've just found 10,000 ways that won't work." —Thomas A. Edison

18. "If you don't value your time, neither will others. Stop giving away your time and talents–start charging for it." —Kim Garst

19. "A successful man is one who can lay a firm foundation with the bricks others have thrown at him." —David Brinkley

20. "No one can make you feel inferior without your consent." —Eleanor Roosevelt

21. "The whole secret of a successful life is to find out what is one's destiny to do, and then do it." —Henry Ford

22. "If you're going through hell keep going." —Winston Churchill

23. "The ones who are crazy enough to think they can change the world, are the ones who do." —Anonymous

24. "Don't raise your voice, improve your argument." —Anonymous

25. "What seems to us as bitter trials are often blessings in disguise." —Oscar Wilde

26. "The meaning of life is to find your gift. The purpose of life is to give it away." —Anonymous

27. "The distance between insanity and genius is measured only by success." —Bruce Feirstein

28. "When you stop chasing the wrong things, you give the right things a chance to catch you." —Lolly Daskal

29. "I believe that the only courage anybody ever needs is the courage to follow your own dreams." —Oprah Winfrey

30. "No masterpiece was ever created by a lazy artist." —Anonymous

31. "Happiness is a butterfly, which when pursued, is always beyond your grasp, but which, if you will sit down quietly, may alight upon you." —Nathaniel Hawthorne

32. "If you can't explain it simply, you don't understand it well enough." —Albert Einstein

33. "Blessed are those who can give without remembering and take without forgetting." —Anonymous

34. "Do one thing every day that scares you." —Anonymous

35. "What's the point of being alive if you don't at least try to do something remarkable." —Anonymous

36. "Life is not about finding yourself. Life is about creating yourself." —Lolly Daskal

37. "Nothing in the world is more common than unsuccessful people with talent." —Anonymous

38. "Knowledge is being aware of what you can do. Wisdom is knowing when not to do it." —Anonymous

39. "Your problem isn't the problem. Your reaction is the problem." —Anonymous

40. "You can do anything, but not everything. —Anonymous

41. "Innovation distinguishes between a leader and a follower." —Steve Jobs

42. "There are two types of people who will tell you that you cannot make a difference in this world: those who are afraid to try and those who are afraid you will succeed." —Ray Goforth

43. "Thinking should become your capital asset, no matter whatever ups and downs you come across in your life." —A.P.J. Abdul Kalam

44. "I find that the harder I work, the more luck I seem to have." —Thomas Jefferson

45. "The starting point of all achievement is desire." —Napoleon Hill

46. "Success is the sum of small efforts, repeated day-in and day-out." —Robert Collier

47. "If you want to achieve excellence, you can get there today. As of this second, quit doing less-

than-excellent work." —Thomas J. Watson

48. "All progress takes place outside the comfort zone." —Michael John Bobak

49. "You may only succeed if you desire succeeding; you may only fail if you do not mind failing." —Philippos

50. "Courage is resistance to fear, mastery of fear–not absence of fear." —Mark Twain

51. "Only put off until tomorrow what you are willing to die having left undone." —Pablo Picasso

52. "People often say that motivation doesn't last. Well, neither does bathing–that's why we recommend it daily." –Zig Ziglar

53. "We become what we think about most of the time, and that's the strangest secret." —Earl Nightingale

54. "The only place where success comes before work is in the dictionary." —Vidal Sassoon

55. "Too many of us are not living our dreams because we are living our fears. " —Les Brown

56. "I find that when you have a real interest in life and a curious life, that sleep is not the most important thing." —Martha Stewart

57. "It's not what you look at that matters, it's what you see." —Anonymous

58. "The road to success and the road to failure are almost exactly the same." —Colin R. Davis

59. "The function of leadership is to produce more leaders, not more followers." —Ralph Nader

60. "Success is liking yourself, liking what you do, and liking how you do it." —Maya Angelou

61. "As we look ahead into the next century, leaders will be those who empower others." —Bill Gates

62. "A real entrepreneur is somebody who has no safety net underneath them." —Henry Kravis

63. "The first step toward success is taken when you refuse to be a captive of the environment in which you first find yourself." —Mark Caine

64. "People who succeed have momentum. The more they succeed, the more they want to succeed, and the more they find a way to succeed. Similarly, when someone is failing, the tendency is to get on a downward spiral that can even become a self-fulfilling prophecy." —Tony Robbins

65. "When I dare to be powerful, to use my strength in the service of my vision, then it becomes less and less important whether I am afraid." —Audre Lorde

66. "Whenever you find yourself on the side of the majority, it is time to pause and reflect." —Mark Twain

67. "The successful warrior is the average man, with laser-like focus." —Bruce Lee

68. "There is no traffic jam along the extra mile." —Roger Staubach

69. "Develop success from failures. Discouragement and failure are two of the surest stepping stones to success." —Dale Carnegie

70. "If you don't design your own life plan, chances are you'll fall into someone else's plan. And guess what they have planned for you? Not much." —Jim Rohn

71. "If you genuinely want something, don't wait for it–teach yourself to be impatient." —Gurbaksh Chahal

72. "Don't let the fear of losing be greater than the excitement of winning." —Robert Kiyosaki

73. "If you want to make a permanent change, stop focusing on the size of your problems and start focusing on the size of you!" —T. Harv Eker

74. "You can't connect the dots looking forward; you can only connect them looking backwards. So you have to trust that the dots will somehow connect in your future. You have to trust in something–your gut, destiny, life, karma, whatever. This approach has never let me down, and it has made all the difference in my life." —Steve Jobs

75. "Two roads diverged in a wood and I took the one less traveled by, and that made all the difference." —Robert Frost

76. "The number one reason people fail in life is because they listen to their friends, family, and neighbors." —Napoleon Hill

77. "The reason most people never reach their goals is that they don't define them, or ever seriously consider them as believable or achievable. Winners can tell you where they are going, what they plan to do along the way, and who will be sharing the adventure with them." —Denis Waitley

78. "In my experience, there is only one motivation, and that is desire. No reasons or principle contain it or stand against it." —Jane Smiley

79. "Success does not consist in never making mistakes but in never making the same one a second time." —George Bernard Shaw

80. "I don't want to get to the end of my life and find that I lived just the length of it. I want to have lived the width of it as well." —Diane Ackerman

81. "You must expect great things of yourself before you can do them." —Michael Jordan

82. "Motivation is what gets you started. Habit is what keeps you going." —Jim Ryun

83. "People rarely succeed unless they have fun in what they are doing." —Dale Carnegie

84. "There is no chance, no destiny, no fate, that can hinder or control the firm resolve of a determined soul." —Ella Wheeler Wilcox

85. "Our greatest fear should not be of failure but of succeeding at things in life that don't really matter." —Francis Chan

86. "You've got to get up every morning with determination if you're going to go to bed with satisfaction." —George Lorimer

87. "A goal is not always meant to be reached; it often serves simply as something to aim at." —Bruce Lee

88. "Success is ... knowing your purpose in life, growing to reach your maximum potential, and sowing seeds that benefit others." —John C. Maxwell

89. "Be miserable. Or motivate yourself. Whatever has to be done, it's always your

choice." —Wayne Dyer

90. "To accomplish great things, we must not only act, but also dream, not only plan, but also believe." —Anatole France

91. "Most of the important things in the world have been accomplished by people who have kept on trying when there seemed to be no help at all." —Dale Carnegie

92. "You measure the size of the accomplishment by the obstacles you had to overcome to reach your goals." —Booker T. Washington

93. "Real difficulties can be overcome; it is only the imaginary ones that are unconquerable." —Theodore N. Vail

94. "It is better to fail in originality than to succeed in imitation." —Herman Melville

95. "What would you do if you weren't afraid." —Spencer Johnson

96. "Little minds are tamed and subdued by misfortune; but great minds rise above it." —Washington Irving

97. "Failure is the condiment that gives success its flavor." —Truman Capote

98. "Don't let what you cannot do interfere with what you can do." —John R. Wooden

99. "You may have to fight a battle more than once to win it." —Margaret Thatcher

100. "A man can be as great as he wants to be. If you believe in yourself and have the courage, the determination, the dedication, the competitive drive and if you are willing to sacrifice the little things in life and pay the price for the things that are worthwhile, it can be done." —Vince Lombardi

1. The road to success and the road to failure are almost exactly the same. Colin R. Davis

2. You may be disappointed if you fail, but you are doomed if you don't try. Beverly Sills

3. Nature has given us all the pieces required to achieve exceptional wellness and health but has left it to us to put these pieces together. Diane McLaren

4. When you change your thoughts, remember to also change your world. Norman Vincent Peale

5. Someday is not a day of the week. Denise Brennan-Nelson

6. Take the attitude of a student, never be too big to ask questions, never know too much to learn something new. Augustine Og Mandino

7. There are three ways to ultimate success: The first way is to be kind. The second way is to be kind. The third way is to be kind. Mister Rogers

8. Experience is a hard teacher because she gives the test first, the lesson afterward. Vernon Sanders Law

9. It's not about better time management. It's about better life management. Alexandra of The Productivity Zone

10. We don't just sit around and wait for other people. We just make, and we do. Arlan Hamilton

11. Think like a queen. A queen is not afraid to fail. Failure is another stepping stone to

greatness. Oprah Winfrey

12. The thing women have yet to learn is nobody gives you power. You just take it. Roseanne Barr

13. Individual commitment to a group effort—that is what makes teamwork, a company work, a society work, a civilization work. Vince Lombardi

14. Promise yourself to give so much time to the improvement of yourself that you have no time to criticize others. To be too large for worry, too noble for anger, too strong for fear, and too happy to permit the presence of trouble. Christian D. Larson

15. When things go wrong, as they sometimes will, when the road you're trudging seems all uphill, when the funds are low and the debts are high, and you want to smile, but you have to sigh when care is pressing you down a bit, rest, if you must, but don't you quit. John Greenleaf Whittier

16. Life's battles don't always go to the stronger or faster man, but sooner or late the man who wins is the man WHO THINKS HE CAN! Walter

D. Wintle

17. To improve is to change; to be perfect is to change often. Winston Churchill

18. Every great dream begins with a dreamer. Always remember, you have within you the strength, the patience, and the passion to reach for the stars to change the world. Harriet Tubman

19. If you want to fly, you have to give up what weighs you down. Roy T. Bennett

20. Change the way you look at things and the things you look at change. Wayne W. Dyer

21. Anyone can give up; it is the easiest thing in the world to do. But to hold it together when everyone would expect you to fall apart, now that is true strength. Chris Bradford

22. Challenges are what make life interesting and overcoming them is what makes life meaningful. Joshua J. Marine

23. It`s not what you say out of your mouth that determines your life, it's what you whisper to yourself that has the most power. Robert T. Kiyosaki

24. Build your own dreams or someone else will hire you to build theirs. Farrah Gray

25. Never give up on a dream just because of the time it will take to accomplish it. The time will pass anyway. Earl Nightingale

26. Every day the clock resets. Your wins don't matter. Your failures don't matter. Don't stress what was, fight for what could be. Sean Higgins

27. You've done it before and you can do it now. See the positive possibilities. Redirect the substantial energy of your frustration and turn it into positive, effective, unstoppable determination. Ralph Marston

28. Every great dream begins with a dreamer. Always remember, you have within you the strength, the patience, and the passion to reach for the stars to change the world. Harriet Tubman

29. When we are no longer able to change a situation, we are challenged to change ourselves. Viktor Frankl

30. I am always ready to learn although I do not always like being taught. Winston Churchill

31. You don't understand anything until you learn it more than one way. Marvin Minsky

32. Develop a passion for learning. If you do, you will never cease to grow. Anthony J. D'Angelo

33. Study hard what interests you the most in the most undisciplined, irreverent, and original manner possible. Richard Feynman

34. Don't let rejection create self-doubt. The founder of Starbucks was turned down by 217 of the 242 investors he initially spoke with. Elizabeth Galbut

35. You will never find time for anything. If you want time you must make it. Charles Buxto

36. Do we need more time? Or do we need to be more disciplined with the time we have? Kerry Johnson

37. You may not control all the events that happen to you, but you can decide not to be reduced by them. Maya Angelou

38. If you think you are too small to make a difference, try sleeping with a mosquito. Dalai Lama

39. The only walls that exist, are those you have placed in your mind. Suzy Kassem

40. It's hard to beat a person who never gives up. Babe Ruth

41. It's okay to be scared. Being scared means you're about to do something really, really brave. Unknown

42. Your time is limited, so don't waste it living someone else's life. Steve Jobs

43. If you want something you've never had, then you've got to do something you've never done. Unknown

44. From small beginnings come great things. Proverb

45. Don't wait. The time will never be just right. Napoleon Hill

46. Sometimes the smallest step in the right direction ends up being the biggest step of your life. Tiptoe if you must, but take the step.

47. Set a goal so big that you can't achieve it until you grow into the person who can.

48. When you know what you want, and want it bad enough, you'll find a way to get it. Jim Rohn

49. Success is walking from failure to failure with no loss of enthusiasm. Winston Churchill

50. Success looks a lot like failure up until the moment you break through the finish line. Dan Waldschmidt

51. At any given moment we have two options: to step forward into growth or step back into safety. Abraham Maslow

52. The ordinary focus on what they're getting. The extraordinary think about who they're becoming.

53. Don't bother telling the world you are ready. Show it. Do it.

54. Start where you are. Use what you have. Do what you can.

55. I never dreamed about success. I worked for it. Estee Lauder

55. Luck is a dividend of sweat. The more you sweat, the luckier you get. Ray Kroc

Hard Work Always Pays Off Quotes

56. Life has two rules: #1 Never quit #2 Always remember rule #1.

57. Many of life's failures are experienced by people who did not realize how close they were to success when they gave up. Thomas Edison

58. You've got to get up every morning with determination if you're going to go to bed with satisfaction. George Lorimer

59. The individual who says it is not possible should move out of the way of those doing it. Tricia Cunningham

60. Make each day your masterpiece. John Wooden

61. The only way to do great work is to love what you do. If you haven't found it yet, keep looking. Don't settle. Steve Jobs

62. Even if you're on the right track, you'll get run over if you just sit there. Will Rogers

63. Success is the sum of small efforts repeated day in and day out. Robert Collier

64. Who you are tomorrow begins with what you do today. Tim Fargo

65. Success is a state of mind. If you want success, start thinking of yourself as a success. Joyce Brothers

66. Concentrate all your thoughts upon the work in hand. The sun's rays do not burn until brought to a focus. Alexander Graham Bell

67. The only place where success comes before work is in the dictionary. Vidal Sassoon

68. The only difference between success and failure is the ability to take action. Alexander Graham Bell

69. Push yourself because no one else is going to do it for you.

70. Success doesn't just find you. You have to go out and get it.

71. The harder you work for something, the greater you'll feel when you achieve it.

72. If people are doubting how far you can go, go so far that you can't hear them anymore. Michele Ruiz

73. Stop being afraid of what could go wrong and think of what could go right.

74. Discipline is doing what needs to be done, even if you don't want to.

75. Work while they sleep. Learn while they party. Save while they spend. Live as they dream.

76. Hustle until you no longer need to introduce yourself.

77. Write it. Shoot it. Publish it. Crochet it, sauté it, whatever. MAKE. Joss Whedon

78. If something is important enough, even if the odds are stacked against you, you should still do it. Elon Musk

79. Things may come to those who wait, but only the things left by those who hustle. Abraham Lincoln

80. The pain you feel today will be the strength you feel tomorrow.

81. Invest in your dreams. Grind now. Shine later.

82. Hustlers don't sleep, they nap.

83. Work hard in silence, let your success be the noise. Frank Ocean

84. Hard work beats talent when talent doesn't work hard. Tim Notke

85. Never stop doing your best just because someone doesn't give you credit. Kamari aka Lyrikal

86. Work hard for what you want because it won't come to you without a fight. You have to be strong and courageous and know that you can do anything you put your mind to. Leah LaBelle

87. Work hard, be kind, and amazing things will happen. Conan O'Brien

88. Set a goal that makes you want to jump out of bed in the morning.

89. Amateurs sit around and wait for inspiration. The rest of us just get up and go to work. Stephen King

90. Success is no accident. It is hard work, perseverance, learning, studying, sacrifice, and most of all, love of what you are doing or learning to do.

91. Focus on being productive instead of busy. Tim Ferriss

92. The elevator to success is out of order. You'll have to use the stairs, one step at a time. Joe Girard

93. By working faithfully eight hours a day you may eventually get to be boss and work twelve hours a day. Robert Frost

94. The road to success is dotted with many tempting parking spaces. Will Rogers

95. Failure is the condiment that gives success its flavor. Truman Capote

96. Be willing to sacrifice what you think you have today for the life that you want tomorrow. Neil Strauss

97. There are no secrets to success. It is the result of preparation, hard work, and learning from failure. Collin Powel

98. Do or do not. There is no try. Yoda

99. There is no time for cut-and-dried monotony. There is time for work. And time for love. That

leaves no other time. Coco Chanel

100. If you love your work, you'll be out there every day trying to do it the best you possibly can, and pretty soon everybody around will catch the passion from you – like a fever. Sam Walton

“Life has to be given a meaning because of the obvious fact that it has no meaning.”

Henry Miller

“I believe that I am not responsible for the meaningfulness or meaninglessness of life, but that I am responsible for what I do with the life I’ve got.”

Hermann Hesse

“If there is meaning in life at all, then there must be meaning in suffering.”

Viktor Frankl

"The literal meaning of life is whatever you're doing that prevents you from killing yourself."

Albert Camus

"Life has no meaning. Each of us has meaning and we bring it to life. It is a waste to be asking the question when you are the answer."

Joseph Campbell

"You will never be happy if you continue to search for what happiness consists of. You will never live if you are looking for the meaning of life."

Albert Camus

"The purpose of life is to stay alive. Watch any animal in nature–all it tries to do is stay alive. It doesn't care about beliefs or philosophy. Whenever any animal's behavior puts it out of touch with the realities of its existence, it becomes exinct."

Michael Crichton

"A life of short duration...could be so rich in joy and love that it could contain more meaning than a life lasting eighty years."

Victor Frankl

"Life is meaningless, when we take a life we take nothing of value."

Brent Weeks

"In order to lead a meaningful life, you need to cherish others, pay attention to human values and try to cultivate inner peace."

Dalai Lama

"Everyone now knows how to find the meaning of life within himself."

Kurt Vonnegut

"Philosophers can debate the meaning of life, but you need a Lord who can declare the meaning of life."

Max Lucado

"So if you want to know the truth about the universe, about the meaning of life, and about your own identity, the best place to start is by observing suffering and exploring what it is. The answer isn't a story."

Yuval Noah Harari

"Ye know full well that the meaning of life is to find your gift. To find your gift is happiness. Never tae find it is misery."

Terry Pratchett

"Each man must look to himself to teach him the meaning of life. It is not something discovered: it is something molded."

Charles Sainte-Beuve

"Life has a meaning but do not set out to find out. Just live it out."

Bangambiki Habyarimana

"Life – a meaningless thing, draped in some moments, that can be given any title or definition."

Neeraj Agnihotri

"We create a meaningful life by what we accept as true and by what we create in the pursuit of truth, love, beauty, and adoration of nature."

Kilroy J. Oldster

"The meanings of life aren't inherited. What is inherited is the mandate to make meanings of life by how we live. The endings of life give life's meanings a chance to show. The beginning of the end of our order, our way, is now in view. This isn't punishment, any more than dying is a punishment for being born."

Stephen Jenkinson

"A man is never an individual unless he is possessed by a desire so deep that it is deeper than life, so deep that he is ready to sacrifice his life for it."

Osho

"Many find in sex and economics the meaning of life and the reason of it all. The consequence of this is that the goal of life for many has become a relief of tension."

Sachindra Kumar Majumdar

"Your life would never have a meaning if you don't have a goal or purpose"

Sunday Adelaja

"A life without concrete product is a meaningless one"

Sunday Adelaja

"Tell me that the purpose of life is to have fun, and without a care in the world I'll begin wreaking havoc on everything I pass. Now that's what I call pure, honest fun."

Criss Jami

"Live is meaningful only if you gave it a meaning."

T. Harv Eker

"If my life had no meaning there was no reason not to end it."

Dan Wells

"Just say up on the hill is the meaning of life and someone knew it and they wanted everyone else to enjoy it. So they put a red vinyl sofa up there."

Melina Marchetta

"There is no purpose to life, you are here to achieve nothing. Whatever you feel is your supreme goal in life is a fiction created by you and the society you are living in, just to keep yourself busy in this purposeless creation.

You are born to die, everything else is pure nonsense."

Anupam S Shlok

"Trying to understand the meaning of life in terms of the human brain's activities is like trying to understand the ocean by going to the shore and scooping out a bucket of water and analyzing it."

Brad Warner

"We can teach our children anything but if we fail to teach them that the meaning of life is first and foremost companionship otherwise known as friendship and love we have failed them as educators."

Wald Wassermann

"Continually looking for the meaning of life is like looking for the meaning of toast. It is sometimes better just to eat the toast."

Matt Haig

"I believe that the meaning of life is to live a life of meaning."

Ken Steven

"Philosophers used to speculate about what they called the meaning of life. (That is now the job of mystics and comedians.)"

Ronald Dworkin

"To find a meaning or to create a meaning; there is no crucial difference as long as it takes away the unpleasant odors of the mortal existence."

Giannis Delimitsos

"We give meaning to life based on our point of view. Only wisdom, like the light of the candle, can bring us a complete view of existence. The key to wisdom is doubt! If you doubted a little, you would definitely be less arrogant."

Marjane Satrapi

"Life is not the word."

Abhijit Naskar

"I feel that my life is devoid of meaning and I no longer see any reason in the acts I perform or the words I say, and it astonishes me that other people can move about outside this nightmare of mine... that they can act and speak."

Luigi Pirandello

"Consider that when you give meaning to everything you see, nothing new can enter your awareness."

Shelley Klammer

"Life is meaningless when you're dead. Meaning can only be had while you live."

A. Aures Garrido

"Your life has no more meaning than what you give to it"

Bangambiki Habyarimana

"If you want to live a meaningful life, start with helping someone, teaching someone, making someone smile, and helping someone heal. Life is meaningful when we help each other walk together."

Aiyaz Uddin

"The meaning of life is something we answer with our own activities, there's no general answer–we determine what the meaning of it is. Meaning in the sense of significance, not in the sense of 'chair means this', but the significance

of your life, is something you create"

Noam Chomsky

"The purpose of your life is Joy. Your objective is to seek joy. Your objective is to find appreciation or pleasure or positive thought from wherever you stand, no matter how you got there. And when you align with that Energy, you are fulfilling your purpose."

Esther Hicks

"To find meaning in life is to know your mission."

Lailah Gifty Akita

"Purpose is finding significance in something so astronomically insignificant."

Viktor Tatarczuk

"A man's mission gives him meaning for living."

Lailah Gifty Akita

"Just when I discovered the meaning of life they change it, just when I'm loving life it seems to start raining."

Mike Skinner

"If you ask for the true meaning of life and get a story in reply, know that this is the wrong answer. The exact details don't really matter. Any story is wrong, simply for being a story. The universe just does not work like a story."

Yuval Noah Harari

"What was the purpose, the meaning, the reason for your life; these are questions for here and now, not for when your time is almost over while waiting for the light to fade."

Steven Redhead

"People have't found meaning in their lives so they're running all the time looking for it."

Mitch Albom

"You don't find your purpose, you choose your purpose..."

Alejandro De la Parra Solomon

"And this nothing, this everything, cannot give life a meaning, but it nonetheless makes life persevere in what it is: a state of non-suicide."

Emil M. Cioran

"When you are fulfilling the meaning of your life, your steps are assertive, but when you are after power or pleasure, you become aggressive."

Roumen Bezergianov,

"What you get when you try to understand the meaning of life intellectually is just one tiny slice of life. Even if you understand that tiny

slice very thoroughly, you still won't really have understood the fullness of life."

Brad Warner

"If you have struggled for a penny then you have understood the true meaning of Life!"

Somya Kedia

"Sometimes the meaning in life hits you like a meteorite."

Curtis Tyrone Jones

"Happiness is the meaning and goal of life. "

Swami Dhyan Giten

"The meaning of life is a "two-way street"—we have the right to expect certain things from life and strive towards them, but it is not over when we are no longer able to expect anything because life still expects things from us."

Roumen Bezergianov

"We all have a passion in life be it writing, singing, dancing, painting, traveling, acting, cooking, modelling, helping the needy, taking photographs, or playing sports; we must always love our passion and make it our sole purpose in life!"

Avijeet Das

9 798887 042541

Printed by Libri Plureos GmbH in Hamburg,
Germany